I0019291

Intellectual Enlightenment

The Transformation from Consumer of Information to Curator of Knowledge

Authored by Alexious Fiero

Copyright

Intellectual Enlightenment: The Transformation from Consumer of Information to Curator of Knowledge

ISBN: 979-8-2816-7685-4
Publisher: Peach Wiz, Inc.
Publishing Platform: Intellectual Enlightenment Magazine
Publishing Website: https://intellectual-enlightenment.com
First Edition | April 2025
Printed in the United States of America

Contact:
Peach Wiz, Inc.
https://peachwiz.com

Epigraph

"Information has become a currency—and it is manipulated as such. The proficiency in the exchange of this currency guarantees success, and every development in humanity and technology should be geared towards optimizing this exchange."

— Alexious Fiero

About the Author

Alexious Fiero is a visionary thinker, strategist, and digital architect of the mind. As the creator of HASE.ai (Human AI Synergy Evangelist), he is leading a new era of cognitive evolution, where artificial intelligence and human intellect converge to foster clarity, creativity, and conscious transformation.

Fiero's work bridges the philosophical and the practical. Drawing from technology, education, and systems design, he equips individuals with the tools and mindsets to navigate the modern information age with wisdom. His passion lies in empowering others to move beyond passive consumption and become intentional curators of knowledge, identity, and legacy.

Known for his ability to synthesize complex ideas into practical insights, Alexious inspires a global audience of learners, creators, and leaders. He is a catalyst for those who seek not only to stay informed—but to think deeply, act ethically, and lead meaningfully.

In *Intellectual Enlightenment*, Fiero shares his most profound vision yet: a roadmap for reclaiming the mind and redefining our future through the power of curated consciousness.

Table of Contents

Part I: The Problem and the Awakening

- The psychology of scrolling

- Algorithmic addiction and cognitive fragmentation

- Why information without intention is intellectual junk food

- Symptoms of passive consumption in daily life

Part II: The Curator's Mindset and Method

4. **Chapter 3: Awakening the Inner Curator**

   - The mindset shift: from sponge to sculptor

   - The power of curiosity with discernment

   - The art of asking better questions

   - Case studies: people who curate for meaning

5. **Chapter 4: Tools of the Curator**

   - Knowledge graphing and second brains

   - Building a Personal Intellectual Operating System (PIOS)

   - Curating across domains: how polymaths think

   - Digital minimalism and intentional input

6. **Chapter 5: The Ethics of Curation**

   ○ Truth vs. narrative: responsibility in sharing

   ○ Fighting misinformation and bias

   ○ The curator's role in the age of AI

   ○ The line between influence and indoctrination

Part III: Sharing, Stewardship, and Legacy

7. **Chapter 6: Teaching is Curation**

   ○ Why teaching is the final form of learning

   ○ Turning knowledge into community impact

   ○ Content creation as intellectual stewardship

   ○ Becoming a signal in the noise

8. **Chapter 7: The Curator's Legacy**

   ○ What future generations will inherit

   ○ Documenting your curated insights

   ○ Curating not just knowledge, but values

   ○ Your intellectual fingerprint

Conclusion: Enlightenment is a Practice

- Daily rituals of the curator

- Lifelong learning as a spiritual act

- Becoming a lighthouse for others

- HASE.ai and the Human-AI Enlightenment Alliance

Dedication

To humanity—

To the thinkers, seekers, and builders of tomorrow. To the minds that dare to question and the hearts that long to understand. To every soul navigating the noise, craving clarity, and choosing growth.

This is for you, and the next step in our evolution.

Because it is no longer enough to consume—we must curate. In this age of infinite information and finite attention, curation is how we reclaim clarity. It is how we shape signal from noise, depth from distraction. It is how we evolve—not only in what we know, but in how we live and what we leave behind.

Preface

We are living in an age defined by abundance—and ambiguity. We have access to more information than any generation before us, yet clarity seems increasingly elusive. The more we scroll, the less we seem to know. The more we consume, the more we drift from understanding. In this paradox lies both the challenge and the opportunity that inspired this book.

Intellectual Enlightenment began as a personal reckoning. I noticed in myself—and in many around me—a quiet but persistent fatigue, not of the body, but of the mind. It was the exhaustion of endless input without integration, of knowing a little about everything but deeply about nothing. We were not thinking more. We were thinking less. And we were mistaking information for wisdom.

This book is my response to that realization. It is a manifesto, a guide, and a companion for anyone ready to reclaim their mind and rise above the noise. It invites you to move from passive consumption to purposeful curation. From scattered attention to focused synthesis. From follower of content to steward of knowledge.

Along this journey, you'll meet the figure of the curator—not as a profession, but as a practice. A curator is someone who does not simply gather, but connects. Who does not just learn, but teaches. Who does not aim to impress, but to illuminate.

This work is not theoretical. It is urgent and practical. It is an offering to the thinkers, builders, teachers, artists, and visionaries who sense that something more is possible—not just in how we learn, but in how we live.

If you are one of those people, I wrote this book for you.

— **Alexious Fiero**

Intellectual Enlightenment: The Transformation from Consumer of Information to Curator of Knowledge

Introduction: The New Intellectual Awakening

We are standing at the precipice of a new intellectual epoch—one marked not by a scarcity of knowledge, but by its overwhelming abundance. Never before in human history has information been so accessible, so immediate, and so unrelenting. With a tap, a swipe, or a spoken command, we summon data from across the globe, from ancient archives to breaking headlines. Yet, amidst this explosion of access lies a troubling paradox: we are flooded with content, yet thirsting for clarity. Drowning in facts, but starving for meaning.

The digital world has transformed us into perpetual consumers. From sunrise to sundown, we scroll, we click, we watch, and we absorb. Our devices hum like digital pacifiers, feeding us a constant stream of newsfeeds, notifications, podcasts, reels, and comment threads. We consume out of habit, out of boredom, and out of fear of missing out. But this passive consumption comes at a steep price—not in money, but in mental clarity and cognitive freedom. Slowly, insidiously, it dulls our critical edge. It weakens our capacity to distinguish fact from opinion, insight from noise, and wisdom from trivia. We become intellectually malnourished, sedated by the illusion of being informed.

Passive consumption is not neutral. It is a subtle but persistent form of cognitive erosion. It sedates curiosity. It discourages independent inquiry. It conditions us to accept narratives rather than interrogate them. It rewards emotional reaction over analytical reflection. And in doing so, it threatens the very foundation of an informed and conscious society. If we are not vigilant, the flood of information will erode our ability to think deeply and independently.

Yet within this chaos lies a call—a quiet, urgent whisper to awaken. To reject the hypnotic rhythm of endless scrolling and reclaim the active power of discerning thought. This is the call to intellectual enlightenment. Not a lofty abstraction reserved for monks and philosophers in secluded towers, but a practical, daily transformation that each of us can undertake. It is a mindset shift, a personal renaissance, a conscious awakening.

To be intellectually enlightened is to become intentional with what we know, how we know it, and how we share it. It is to think in systems, to seek depth over volume, and to embrace nuance over simplicity. It means living not just informed, but aligned. It requires discernment, patience, and a willingness to unlearn as much as we learn. It challenges us to take responsibility for our intellectual ecosystems.

And from this call emerges a new figure—an archetype for our age—the Curator.

The Curator is not merely a collector of facts or a regurgitator of data, but an alchemist of meaning. They are part scholar, part philosopher, part storyteller. They sift through noise with surgical precision. They connect seemingly unrelated dots into elegant patterns of understanding. They organize chaos into coherence. They teach not to perform, but to illuminate. They write not to impress, but to empower. In a world drowning in information, the Curator becomes a beacon of knowledge—sharp, grounded, purposeful, and deeply human.

The Curator does not consume reactively; they engage intentionally. They don't just read—they synthesize. They don't just store data—they weave it into context. They are bridge-builders between knowledge and wisdom, between content and consciousness. They embody the possibility of a new kind of thinker—one who values quality over quantity, clarity over popularity, and wisdom over virality.

This book is your guide, your manifesto, and your roadmap for that transformation. It is for the thinkers, the skeptics, the truth-seekers, and the silent observers ready to speak. It is for overstimulated minds that crave focus, for learners who hunger for depth, and for creators weary of echo chambers, yearning for authentic insight. It is for anyone who senses there is more to knowing than consuming— that there is a deeper, richer, more luminous way to engage with the world of ideas.

Welcome to the New Intellectual Awakening.
Welcome to the rise of the Curator.
Welcome to your evolution.

Chapter 1: The Age of Information Glut

The Evolution of Human Knowledge Transmission

Human history can be mapped through the revolutions in how we transmit, preserve, and interact with information. In the beginning, knowledge lived only in memory and voice. The **oral tradition** was our first library—stories, songs, and wisdom passed from one generation to the next around fires and within families. It was a fragile, communal system—deeply human, but easily lost. It relied on repetition, ritual, and the collective memory of the tribe. Knowledge was embedded in culture, ceremonies, and myth. It was preserved through performance, not paper.

Then came the **written word**, and with it, the ability to preserve thoughts beyond the lifespan of a single person. Clay tablets, scrolls, and codices gave rise to a new era—where scribes, monks, and scholars became stewards of civilization's memory. Writing externalized thought, freeing it from the limits of memory and geography. But access remained scarce. Books were rare, and literacy was a privilege. Knowledge belonged to the few—religious leaders, aristocrats, and academics—who controlled what was recorded, copied, and transmitted.

The **printing press** changed that. Gutenberg's invention in the 15th century democratized access to information. Books became widespread, ideas crossed borders, and revolutions—in science, politics, and philosophy—ignited across Europe. The printing press was not merely a technological innovation—it was a cultural detonation. It enabled the spread of ideas at scale and speed previously unimagined. Knowledge was no longer the property of the elite. It was becoming a public force.

Fast forward to the **digital age**, and the internet becomes the latest, most explosive revolution of all. Suddenly, information is not just accessible—it is inescapable. Search engines replaced libraries, blogs rivaled newspapers, and everyone became both reader and publisher. Knowledge went viral. Smartphones put the sum of human knowledge in our pockets. With a few keystrokes, we can retrieve medical advice, philosophical treatises, cooking tips, or global news. But with this unprecedented access came a new set of challenges. We moved from an age of information scarcity to one of overwhelming abundance.

From Scarcity to Excess

For most of history, the problem was not having enough information. Now, the problem is having too much. We have crossed a threshold from **informational scarcity** to **informational excess**—from famine to flood.

This abundance, paradoxically, has not led to clarity, but confusion. With so many voices, platforms, and perspectives competing for our attention, the signal-to-noise ratio has collapsed. Every topic has a thousand takes. Every question has ten thousand answers. And so, we begin to lose the ability to discern not just what is true, but what is *worth knowing*.

We live in an era where content is king—but coherence is missing. In this environment, **quality** suffers. Speed outpaces accuracy. Virality trumps veracity. Content is optimized not for depth, but for clicks. The race is not for truth, but for attention. And in this chaotic ecosystem, the individual must learn to filter or be overwhelmed. We are left with the illusion of knowledge—a surface-level familiarity that lacks understanding.

The transformation from scarcity to excess demands a new literacy: the ability to **discern**, **filter**, and **curate**. It's no longer enough to access information; we must know how to navigate, contextualize, and evaluate it. Without these skills, we become overwhelmed, misinformed, or manipulated.

Attention: The New Currency

In the digital economy, **attention** is the most valuable resource. Not oil. Not gold. Not even data. Attention is what platforms fight for, what algorithms mine, and what advertisers monetize.

Every ping, every notification, every trending headline is an attempt to capture your gaze—for a second longer, a scroll further, a click deeper. But attention is finite. We have only so many minutes in a day, only so much focus to give. And when our attention is constantly fragmented, our capacity for deep thinking, critical analysis, and creative insight erodes.

This economy incentivizes **distraction**, not reflection. The faster the feed, the less time we have to digest. The more we consume, the less we remember. In a world engineered for engagement, depth becomes a casualty. This leads to what some researchers call "continuous partial attention"—a state where we are constantly monitoring multiple streams of information, but rarely diving deeply into any of them.

The implications are profound. Shallow attention leads to shallow understanding. We mistake familiarity for mastery. We skim headlines and call it news. We read summaries and assume expertise. Our intellectual muscles atrophy from lack of rigorous use.

To thrive in this environment, we must reclaim our attention as a sacred resource. We must protect it from manipulation, anchor it in purpose, and use it intentionally. Attention is the gateway to insight—and we must treat it as such.

The Paradox of Access

More information does not automatically lead to more understanding. In fact, the more we know, the harder it becomes to organize, prioritize, and contextualize what matters. This is the great **paradox of access**: we live in the most informed era in history, yet many feel more confused, more anxious, and more intellectually paralyzed than ever before.

This paradox challenges the myth that technology alone will liberate us. Tools are only as powerful as the hands that wield them. The problem isn't the availability of information—it's the **lack of frameworks, filters**, and **foundations** for turning that information into wisdom.

We must become intentional architects of our intellectual environments. That means creating systems to capture, connect, and contextualize what we learn. It means building personal knowledge networks and adopting tools that help us make sense, not just take in. It means being less reactive and more reflective, less scattered and more structured.

In this new reality, the role of the **Curator** emerges as essential. The Curator doesn't just navigate the flood—they build bridges across it. They organize, discern, and elevate. They help others make sense of the world by first making sense of it themselves. They are intellectual guides in a landscape of chaos.

As we move forward, the ability to curate knowledge—to structure it meaningfully, to apply it wisely, and to share it responsibly—may become the most important intellectual skill of the 21st century. Curation is not just a personal tool; it's a social responsibility. In a world where anyone can publish, the need for thoughtful editors, synthesizers, and translators of knowledge has never been greater.

Welcome to the Age of Information Glut.
Welcome to the age where curation is not just helpful—it is survival.

Chapter 2: The Passive Consumer

The Psychology of Scrolling

It begins innocently. A moment of downtime. A quick glance at your phone. You open your favorite app—just for a minute. But minutes stretch into an hour. The feed pulls you in, one post leading to the next. By the time you look up, you barely remember what you saw, only that you saw a lot of it. This is the psychology of scrolling: a continuous partial engagement designed to feel effortless and addictive.

Our brains are hardwired to seek novelty, to respond to stimulation. Every swipe offers a tiny reward—an image, a meme, a headline, a notification. Dopamine, the brain's pleasure chemical, is released in anticipation of what comes next. We are hooked not by content itself, but by the possibility of what might be just beyond the next scroll. It is a digital slot machine, with our focus as the jackpot.

This cycle of intermittent rewards, pioneered in behavioral psychology, is precisely what keeps us tethered to our devices. We are not just consuming—we are being conditioned. Every micro-hit of dopamine strengthens a habit loop. We seek, we swipe, we see, and we start over. Over time, this becomes less a choice and more a reflex. We check our devices not because we need information, but because we crave stimulation.

Algorithmic Addiction and Cognitive Fragmentation

Behind every feed is an algorithm. These invisible architects of our attention track what we pause on, what we like, what we share.

Then they optimize for more of the same. Over time, our feeds become echo chambers—reinforcing our biases, narrowing our worldview, and fragmenting our focus.

This algorithmic curation is not neutral. It is engineered to maximize engagement, not understanding. It rewards outrage, sensationalism, and controversy. It buries nuance and elevates emotional reaction. The result? A society overstimulated yet underinformed. Our thoughts become scattered, our attention divided, our conversations shallow.

Cognitive fragmentation sets in. We struggle to concentrate, to follow complex arguments, to sit with ambiguity. Our mental landscape is no longer a deep forest of ideas but a flickering mosaic of disconnected impressions. We consume more but retain less. We skim instead of study. We react rather than reflect.

The result is a dilution of intellectual stamina. We find it harder to engage in sustained thought, to hold conflicting ideas in mind, or to resist the pull of instant gratification. The depth of our thinking erodes, replaced by a compulsion to move on to the next thing—quickly, superficially, and without resolution.

Information Without Intention: Intellectual Junk Food

Information is not inherently nourishing. Like food, its value depends on quality, context, and how it is processed. When we consume without intention—when we scroll without purpose—we ingest intellectual junk food. Empty calories for the mind.

It fills the space but not the soul. It creates the illusion of learning without the substance of understanding. We feel informed because we've read headlines, watched summaries, or glanced at infographics. But without reflection, integration, or synthesis, that information becomes clutter. Noise, not knowledge.

And like junk food, this kind of consumption creates dependency without sustenance. The more we consume, the more we crave. But we rarely feel satisfied. We seek more stimulation, not because we are hungry for truth, but because we are conditioned to avoid silence. This cycle is not just unhealthy—it is unsustainable.

Intentionality is the key difference between consumption and curation. A passive consumer asks, "What's new?" A curator asks, "What's useful? What's true? What fits into the broader picture I'm building in my mind?" The curator resists the dopamine-fueled temptation to binge on headlines and instead builds a thoughtful meal of insight.

Symptoms of Passive Consumption in Daily Life

How can you tell if you're caught in the trap of passive consumption? The symptoms are subtle but pervasive:

- **Mental fatigue**, despite having done little "thinking"

- **Shallow memory** of what you've read, watched, or listened to

- **Shortened attention span**, especially for long-form content

- **Reduced curiosity**, as the algorithm serves content you didn't seek

- **Irritability** or anxiety after extended screen time

- **The compulsion to check** your phone for no particular reason

- **Inability to recall or articulate ideas clearly** after exposure to large amounts of content

- **Loss of intellectual motivation,** making deep learning feel like a chore

Passive consumption creates a cycle. It numbs curiosity, which reduces engagement, which leads to more passive intake. Breaking that cycle requires awareness, discipline, and a reorientation of habits. It demands that we pause and question not just what we're consuming, but *why* we are consuming it. What are we hoping to learn, and how will we use it?

Reclaiming agency over our attention is the first step toward liberation. It begins by treating our minds not as dumping grounds, but as sacred spaces—spaces that deserve quality input, intentional reflection, and the nourishing silence that allows true understanding to emerge.

As we move deeper into the digital era, the challenge is not only how much we consume, but how consciously we do it. The next chapter will explore how to shift from this passive state toward a more empowered and intentional role: the awakening of the inner Curator.

Chapter 3: Awakening the Inner Curator

The Mindset Shift: From Sponge to Sculptor

The journey from passive consumer to active curator begins with a fundamental mindset shift. Most people approach knowledge like a sponge—soaking up as much as possible, indiscriminately, with the belief that more is better. But in an age of infinite input, saturation becomes paralysis. Absorbing without processing leads to overload, not insight.

To become a curator, we must shift from sponge to **sculptor**. A sculptor does not collect every piece of stone. They choose deliberately. They carve, refine, and shape raw material into something meaningful. Likewise, a curator of knowledge chooses what to engage with, filters with intention, and connects ideas to build a coherent worldview. This transformation marks the awakening of the inner curator—an identity rooted in purpose, discernment, and synthesis.

Curators don't hoard information. They organize it. They don't just gather facts; they contextualize and elevate them. The curator is not a vessel of facts but a vessel of *meaning*—a creator of mental architecture rather than a collector of intellectual artifacts. This process isn't passive or automatic—it requires intellectual courage, emotional patience, and a deep commitment to truth-seeking.

Curators also accept that knowledge is never complete. They live in the tension between certainty and curiosity. They understand that curation is an ongoing act of refinement—a process that involves selecting what aligns with one's values, questioning what doesn't, and discarding what no longer serves clarity.

The Power of Curiosity with Discernment

Curiosity is the engine of the curator's mind. But not all curiosity is equal. **Curiosity with discernment** is what separates the truly enlightened thinker from the eternally distracted browser. It's the kind of curiosity that goes beyond "What happened?" to ask, "Why does this matter? What patterns does this reveal? What can be learned, applied, or challenged?"

Discernment is what keeps curiosity grounded. Without it, curiosity becomes scattershot, pulled in every direction by the latest trend or notification. Discernment is the filter that prioritizes quality over quantity, relevance over novelty, and depth over breadth. It enables us to say no to the noise and yes to what truly enriches our minds.

Together, curiosity and discernment form the core of intellectual self-governance. They empower the curator to navigate the ocean of content with clarity and direction. They allow the mind to remain open, yet not gullible; engaged, yet not overwhelmed.

Curiosity with discernment also fosters intellectual humility. The best curators understand that no single source, idea, or framework has all the answers. They approach their quest for knowledge not as a pursuit of finality, but for greater resolution. They see ideas not as static truths but as evolving perspectives to be explored, tested, and refined over time.

The Art of Asking Better Questions

Curation begins with the right questions. The quality of your questions determines the quality of your insights. Passive consumers ask surface-level questions: "What's happening?" or "What's popular?" Curators ask transformative questions:

- "What is the underlying principle here?"

- "How does this connect to what I already know?"

- "What perspective is missing from this narrative?"

- "What actions or decisions could this knowledge inform?"

These are questions that don't just seek answers—they seek *understanding*. They open doors rather than close them. They foster humility because they acknowledge complexity. They turn content into context.

Great curators are relentless questioners. They challenge assumptions, spot contradictions, and trace threads across disciplines. They develop a radar for relevance and a habit of reflecting, not just reacting. In doing so, they sharpen both their insight and their influence.

Furthermore, the habit of better questioning nurtures adaptability. In a world where information changes rapidly, it is not the memorizer who thrives, but the interrogator—the one who can analyze, synthesize, and reframe. Better questions are the compass that guides us through the complexity of modern knowledge.

Case Studies: People Who Curate for Meaning

Throughout history and into the modern era, we find powerful examples of individuals who embody the curator's mindset:

- **Leonardo da Vinci**, the quintessential polymath, curated knowledge across art, anatomy, mechanics, and nature—not for fame, but for a holistic understanding of life. His notebooks are masterpieces of interdisciplinary curiosity. He drew no boundary between science and art, believing both emerged from keen observation and connected thinking.

- **Maria Popova**, creator of *The Marginalian* (formerly *Brain Pickings*), synthesizes literature, philosophy, science, and art into insightful essays that connect timeless ideas to the modern soul. She doesn't chase trends—she traces meaning, offering slow journalism in an age of instant opinion.

- **Ryan Holiday**, author and modern Stoic, curates classical philosophy for contemporary life. He filters the chaos of modern culture through timeless truths, helping readers apply ancient wisdom to everyday challenges. His newsletters, books, and daily meditations exemplify the role of the curator as translator across time.

- **Austin Kleon**, through his books like *Steal Like an Artist*, champions the idea of creative curation—gathering influence with intention, remixing knowledge into original insight, and openly sharing the process. He turns inspiration into action, revealing how curation fuels creativity.

- **Tim Ferriss**, known for his ability to distill complex systems into practical life strategies, curates wisdom from top performers across disciplines. His podcast and writing exemplify high-level synthesis and the power of targeted inquiry.

These individuals exemplify the shift from mindless consumption to mindful curation. They show that curation is not about elitism or expertise—it's about integrity, intention, and impact. It's about choosing quality over noise, meaning over momentum.

The Curator's Identity and Discipline

Awakening the inner curator is not just about managing information—it's about shaping identity. It's about becoming the architect of your intellectual landscape. It's a daily discipline, a worldview, and a quiet revolution against intellectual inertia. It is the work of building a meaningful life through meaningful learning.

In the next chapter, we'll explore the tools and systems that empower this transformation and support the practice of lifelong curation—tools that act not as substitutes for thinking, but as amplifiers of reflection, retention, and clarity.

Chapter 4: Tools of the Curator

Designing the Architecture of Insight

Curation requires more than good habits—it demands intelligent, personalized systems. In an age where data flows like water, the modern curator must learn not merely to collect, but to **contain and connect**. This is where the concept of the **second brain** becomes transformative—a digital extension of your mind, designed to capture, store, and activate ideas with strategic, long-term value.

Knowledge Graphing and Second Brains

Platforms like **Notion, Obsidian,** and **Roam Research** have emerged as essential tools for building a second brain. These applications allow for the creation of **knowledge graphs**—networks of interlinked ideas that mirror the brain's natural associative pathways. Unlike rigid folder structures, knowledge graphs empower you to visualize how concepts relate, evolve, and catalyze deeper understanding.

Obsidian and **Roam** excel in bi-directional linking, turning your notes into living networks where past reflections converge with present insights. **Notion**, with its balance of structure and customization, is ideal for integrating tasks, databases, and documents into one cohesive ecosystem. Together, these tools form the digital foundation for thoughtful, interconnected knowledge.

A second brain is more than digital storage—it is a **thinking environment**. It becomes your personal knowledge lab: a space where curiosity meets clarity. Within it, fragmented ideas are revisited and refined, inspiration is archived for future projects, and patterns emerge that deepen understanding. You no longer fear forgetting, because your system remembers *for* you—organized in your unique intellectual language.

Building a Personal Intellectual Operating System (PIOS)

While tools are valuable, they're only as effective as the system behind them. This is where the **Personal Intellectual Operating System (PIOS)** becomes essential. A PIOS is the integrated framework by which you manage knowledge—across four dynamic stages: **input, processing, output, and review**.

- **Input**: Capture insights from books, podcasts, conversations, experiences, and observations. Be selective about what enters your system.

- **Processing**: Reflect on, annotate, and connect your inputs. This stage turns passive information into active insight.

- **Output**: Apply your understanding through writing, speaking, designing, teaching, or decision-making. Knowledge is refined in use.

- **Review**: Periodically revisit your notes and thoughts to reinforce memory, deepen comprehension, and recontextualize meaning.

A well-designed PIOS is **frictionless, flexible, and personal**. It evolves with your goals, adapts to your rhythms, and transforms chaos into clarity. Over time, it shifts your mental state from reactive to reflective, from overwhelmed to empowered.

Curating Across Domains: How Polymaths Think

The most powerful curators do not confine themselves to a single discipline. Like da Vinci, Franklin, and Angelou, they **transcend boundaries**, weaving wisdom across diverse fields to create new forms of understanding.

To curate across domains, one must:

- Cultivate **interdisciplinary curiosity**.

- Recognize **universal patterns** and metaphors.

- Translate insights across fields for novel problem-solving.

This synthesis expands both creativity and insight. A biological model might inspire a business strategy. A philosophical argument could inform a design principle. Polymathic thinking builds bridges between seemingly unrelated ideas, sparking innovation.

Modern tools amplify this potential. Tagging systems in Obsidian, relational databases in Notion, and backlinking in Roam all support holistic knowledge management. When curated intentionally, your notes become a living archive of cross-domain intelligence—ready to inform projects and decisions in unexpected ways.

Today's global challenges—from climate change to AI ethics— require **systems thinking**. The polymathic curator is uniquely equipped to meet this moment, synthesizing insight across contexts to make informed, multidimensional contributions.

Digital Minimalism and Intentional Input

In a world engineered for distraction, **restraint is power**. The modern curator must not only choose what to include—but also what to exclude. **Digital minimalism** is the practice of designing a digital life that serves your thinking instead of scattering your attention.

Intentional input includes:

- Subscribing only to **signal-rich** sources.

- Establishing **content boundaries** to avoid overwhelm.

- Practicing **rituals of reflection**, such as journaling or mind-mapping, to synthesize what you've absorbed.

Tools like **RSS readers, email filters**, and **read-it-later apps** (e.g., Instapaper, Pocket) support this intentional approach. More than productivity hacks, they are integral to cultivating focus, depth, and discernment.

The minimalist curator is not less informed—they are **precisely informed**. They consume with purpose, absorbing information that aligns with their values and aspirations. In doing so, they reclaim time, clarity, and cognitive sovereignty.

In an era of excess, they choose sufficiency. In a culture of noise, they become a signal.

The tools of the curator—both digital and mental—are not ends in themselves. They are **scaffolding** for a life of meaningful inquiry, purposeful learning, and creative contribution. They help transform raw data into insight, insight into wisdom, and wisdom into legacy.

In the next chapter, we'll explore the ethical responsibilities of the curator in a time when information can empower—or mislead—and how to ensure your voice adds clarity and value to the collective conversation.

Chapter 5: The Ethics of Curation

Upholding Integrity in a World of Infinite Narratives

Truth vs. Narrative: Responsibility in Sharing

With great knowledge comes great responsibility. As curators, we are not merely organizing data—we are shaping perception, culture, and understanding. Every quote, article, study, or insight we choose to share carries weight. It constructs a lens through which others may come to interpret the world. In this light, the act of curation is not neutral—it is deeply ethical and often political.

There is a nuanced tension between **truth** and **narrative**. While facts exist independently, they are rarely consumed in isolation. They are embedded in stories, shaped by context, and framed by intention. A well-selected statistic can either illuminate an issue or distort it depending on how it is presented. A quote taken out of context can radically alter its meaning. The ethical curator must cultivate a sharp sensitivity to these manipulations—not just from external sources, but within themselves.

The ethical curator asks: Is this accurate? Is it full? Is it being presented in a way that fosters understanding or division? They understand that storytelling can educate, inspire, and move hearts—but it can also manipulate, mislead, and divide. Therefore, they strive to provide not only information, but **context**. They avoid the temptation of cherry-picking and instead offer a balanced presentation of complex ideas. They serve **understanding** over persuasion, **clarity** over control.

Fighting Misinformation and Bias

We live in an age where misinformation spreads faster than truth. Falsehoods, designed to incite emotion and engagement, are algorithmically favored. As a result, curators are now on the front lines of an intellectual and cultural battle. They are not only educators—they are **defenders of discourse**.

But misinformation is not only "out there." It also lives **within** us. Our own cognitive biases—confirmation bias, availability bias, tribal thinking—shape how we perceive, interpret, and remember information. Ethical curation requires rigorous self-examination. It begins with the awareness that our minds are not passive vessels, but active filters.

To fight misinformation and bias, curators must:

- Engage in **source vetting** and verify claims with **primary evidence**.

- Consult a **range of perspectives**—including those they disagree with.

- Identify the difference between **fact, analysis, opinion, and speculation**.

- Make room for **doubt**, especially in fast-moving or emotionally charged topics.

Crucially, curators must also model these habits publicly. By transparently disclosing sources, showing how conclusions were reached, and acknowledging areas of uncertainty, they model what ethical information processing looks like. They elevate the conversation and empower others to become critical thinkers.

In doing so, they act as **cultural antibodies**—neutralizing harmful falsehoods not through censorship, but through clarity and courage.

The Curator's Role in the Age of AI

Artificial intelligence has exponentially increased the volume, velocity, and virality of content. Personalized feeds driven by algorithms now shape much of what we consume. AI not only distributes information—it constructs reality for many people. In this rapidly changing environment, the curator's role is more crucial than ever.

We must now act as **conscious mediators** between machine-generated content and human values. AI tools can aid in curation—by organizing, summarizing, and retrieving data—but they also pose ethical challenges. Algorithms prioritize engagement, not enlightenment. They are not neutral; they reflect the biases and incentives of their designers.

Curators in the AI era must:

- Understand how algorithmic systems influence visibility and beliefs.

- Use AI tools critically—as collaborators, not authorities.

- Actively **counteract echo chambers** by introducing diverse, dissenting, and global voices.

- Cultivate **algorithmic awareness**—noticing when content is being shaped more for virality than value.

More importantly, curators must **humanize the digital experience**. They must foreground empathy, context, and wisdom—qualities AI cannot replicate. They must protect the subtle and the slow in a world addicted to the fast and the loud. They must remind us that not everything that matters can be measured.

The Line Between Influence and Indoctrination

Every act of curation exerts **influence**. But influence, when unchecked, can slip into **indoctrination**. The ethical curator walks a narrow bridge between guiding and imposing, between presenting a viewpoint and programming belief.

This is particularly important in an era of ideological polarization. Curators must resist the temptation to become propagandists for a cause—even a noble one. Instead, they must:

- Frame content in a way that **stimulates thinking**, not just agreement.

- Share opposing viewpoints alongside their own with **intellectual generosity**.

- Encourage others to **draw their own conclusions**.

Curators are not preachers. They are **facilitators of reflection**. Their mission is not to convince, but to awaken. They recognize that true empowerment does not come from handing people answers—but from helping them ask better questions.

By holding space for complexity, contradiction, and conversation, ethical curators become **catalysts for understanding**. They transform audiences from passive absorbers into active explorers. They build communities that value thoughtfulness over certainty, dialogue over doctrine.

In the next chapter, we'll explore how curators move from private reflection to public contribution—how teaching, sharing, and storytelling become powerful acts of intellectual leadership and service in a world hungry for authentic, well-framed knowledge.

Chapter 6: Teaching is Curation

Why Teaching Is the Final Form of Learning

There is a timeless truth among educators, philosophers, and knowledge workers: **to teach is to learn twice**. Teaching does not merely communicate knowledge—it consolidates it. It transforms what we know into what we can explain, and what we can explain into what we can embody. Through teaching, knowledge becomes deeply rooted, more nuanced, and more adaptable.

Teaching forces us to confront gaps in our understanding. It demands clarity, structure, empathy, and the ability to see through another's lens. It requires us to distill complexity into coherence and translate abstract concepts into tangible applications. In this way, teaching becomes the ultimate test of comprehension. A concept that we once held vaguely becomes sharp when we must explain it to someone else. A pattern once intuitive becomes intelligible when we diagram it, share it, and translate it into different formats.

The curator who teaches isn't just transmitting facts—they are facilitating transformation. They become a conduit between information and integration, between ideas and implementation. They help others bridge theory with practice and inspire independent thinking. In teaching, curators evolve from knowledge collectors to **knowledge cultivators**—nurturing wisdom in others while refining their own.

Turning Knowledge into Community Impact

Knowledge that lives only in private notes is inert. The true power of curated wisdom is realized when it begins to shape the world around us. Teaching is the medium through which personal insight becomes **public contribution**. It is where internal mastery turns outward to serve collective progress.

When curators share what they've learned—through mentorship, facilitation, workshops, writing, or informal conversations—they amplify the value of their learning. They invite others to build upon it, challenge it, and evolve it. This process transforms knowledge into a **living organism** that adapts and expands through interaction.

They also build bridges between silos—connecting people across disciplines, cultures, and generations. In doing so, they create a **knowledge commons**: a shared intellectual ecosystem that grows richer with every contribution. Communities that embrace this model become more resilient, innovative, and compassionate.

Teaching doesn't have to mean standing in front of a classroom. It can happen in blog posts, podcasts, diagrams, social threads, collaborative documents, or YouTube channels. It can emerge from workshops, roundtables, or even well-phrased questions in a comment thread. What matters is not the format but the **intent**—to serve, to connect, and to elevate.

In this way, curation becomes an act of **community building**. It helps people find their way through complexity. It gives voice to the underexplored. It validates diverse experiences and democratizes access to insight. And it reminds us that wisdom is meant to circulate—not accumulate.

Content Creation as Intellectual Stewardship

In the digital age, content creation is the modern modality of teaching. But it's more than marketing or personal branding—it's

intellectual stewardship. Each article, video, visual map, or podcast episode becomes part of a legacy: a digital artifact that can inform, inspire, or transform someone's path long after it's been created.

Content creators who are also curators hold a higher standard. They:

- Prioritize **depth over virality**.

- Cite **sources** and give credit where it's due.

- Value **original synthesis**, not just repetition.

- Maintain **integrity** over influence.

- Focus on **usefulness** rather than performance metrics.

They act not as entertainers, but as educators—even when the medium is informal. They resist the temptation of clickbait and instead choose content that respects the attention of their audience. They craft messages that are **both timely and timeless**, rooted in curiosity and driven by contribution.

This form of content creation is a service. It's an offering. It's a way of saying, "Here's what I've gathered. Let me show you how it fits, why it matters, and how you might use it." When practiced with care, it becomes a sacred act—a means of transmitting not just data, but wisdom, values, and clarity.

Creators who steward knowledge this way help preserve humanity in the digital landscape. They reintroduce reflection into the stream of reaction. They help audiences pause, think, and feel. And they leave behind a trail not just of content, but of consciousness.

Becoming a Signal in the Noise

In a world flooded with low-resolution thinking and high-volume distraction, the curator who teaches becomes a **signal in the noise**. Their work doesn't just inform—it orients. It doesn't just entertain—it equips. It doesn't just go viral—it goes deep.

To be a signal means:

- Having the **discipline** to publish with purpose, not pressure.

- Having the **humility** to admit what you don't know while celebrating what you've learned.

- Having the **courage** to speak thoughtfully in a loud world where speed is often mistaken for substance.

Being a signal is not about being right. It's about being **clear**, being **honest**, and being **useful**. It's about serving as a beacon for those navigating complexity, confusion, and contradiction. It's about showing others how to think, not just what to think.

Signals don't fade—they resonate. And those who choose to teach as an act of curation don't just inform their audience—they elevate them.

In the final chapter, we'll explore the curator's legacy—how the practice of knowledge stewardship shapes not just the world around us, but the inner architecture of a meaningful, enlightened life.

Chapter 7: The Curator's Legacy

What Future Generations Will Inherit

The decisions we make about what to learn, share, and preserve are not just for our time—they ripple into the future. Every act of curation we engage in today shapes the intellectual and moral landscape of tomorrow. Our notes, reflections, collections, and creations become the **soil of future insight**, the building blocks of wisdom that subsequent generations will either grow from or grow through.

Future generations will not only inherit our technology or culture—they will inherit our **interpretations**, **perspectives**, and **priorities**. What we amplify, what we question, what we protect, and what we choose to forget all signal what we believed mattered. Curation is not merely informational—it is **philosophical, ethical, and profoundly cultural**.

To curate with legacy in mind is to live with intention. It is to serve not only clarity in the present but continuity and relevance in the future. It means asking: What will endure? What wisdom will resonate a century from now? What truths must be safeguarded, even as the world evolves?

Curation is a form of time travel—a bridge between today's insights and tomorrow's civilizations.

Documenting Your Curated Insights

Curation becomes legacy when it is documented and shared in forms others can access, apply, and build upon. A curated insight not externalized is a candle unlit—its flame never passed, its light never seen.

Documenting your insights makes your thinking visible, traceable, and expandable. It transforms your personal learning into communal treasure. Consider these formats:

- A digital **knowledge vault** with your most meaningful and regularly updated notes.

- A curated and annotated **reading list** that reveals not only what you've read but how it shaped your thinking.

- A personal **glossary of principles**, mental models, and axioms that guide your worldview.

- A **timeline of intellectual milestones** showing the evolution of your ideas and what influenced them.

- A **digital garden**—a living, evolving system where insights grow, intertwine, and blossom over time.

The goal is not to impress others with what you know but to leave a clear, nourishing trail for others to follow, adapt, and contribute to. These archives act as both mirrors and maps. They illuminate your journey and help others navigate their own.

Curating Not Just Knowledge, but Values

Curation is never neutral. What we highlight and how we frame it reflects not just what we know, but what we **care about**. Each collection, summary, and synthesis is a declaration of values.

Thus, the curator is more than an organizer of ideas—they are a **moral architect**. They help shape the frameworks through which societies interpret meaning and make decisions. Principles embedded in curation—curiosity, integrity, compassion, nuance, humility—are more than scholarly virtues; they are ingredients of a thriving, ethical civilization.

To curate with ethical intention, ask:

- Is this content promoting empathy or sowing division?

- Is it deepening understanding or exploiting attention?

- Is it empowering others to think or prescribing what to believe?

- Is it timeless, or simply trendy?

When we curate with values at the core, we transcend content creation—we help shape the cultural conditions for wisdom to flourish. In doing so, our curation becomes an **act of stewardship**.

Your Intellectual Fingerprint

Every curator leaves behind a unique signature—a synthesis that no one else can replicate. This is your **intellectual fingerprint**. It reveals itself not only in what you share, but in how you connect, contextualize, and carry ideas forward.

Your intellectual fingerprint includes:

- The pattern of your questions and the clarity of your conclusions.

- The tone and depth of your commentary.

- The coherence of your frameworks and the resonance of your insights.

- The texture of your metaphors, analogies, and interpretations.

No algorithm can replicate this. It is forged through your experiences, your questions, your failures, your insights, and your emotional lens. It is wholly and irreplaceably yours.

By documenting and sharing your intellectual fingerprint, you give others permission to do the same. You model the courage not just to learn—but to be **seen as a learner**. You serve not only as a guide, but as a companion in another's journey toward greater understanding.

As we close this book, remember: you are not merely a consumer of information. You are a **curator of meaning**. And that is no small role—it is a calling, a craft, and a quiet revolution. It is the conscious shaping of knowledge, the pursuit of sense-making, and the courage to pass that light on.

Your legacy is not just what you know—it is what you choose to preserve, refine, and share. It is the clarity you bring to complexity. The signal you send across time.

What you choose to learn, teach, and leave behind will echo.

Let it echo with intention. Let it echo with integrity. Let it echo with wonder.

Conclusion: Enlightenment is a Practice

Daily Rituals of the Curator

The transformation from consumer to curator is not a one-time leap—it is a **daily return**. Enlightenment is not a fixed state but a living process, a constant refining of awareness and wisdom. It is a **practice**, a deliberate rhythm of engagement that turns raw information into integrated insight and learning into empowered leadership. The curator's life is shaped by consistent, mindful rituals:

- **Capture**: Keep a notebook, voice memo, or digital inbox ready to record spontaneous insights, questions, and reflections.

- **Review**: Regularly revisit, refine, and reframe your notes to reinforce learning, recognize connections, and surface dormant ideas.

- **Synthesize**: Transform scattered information into structured frameworks and meaningful narratives that make sense of complexity.

- **Share**: Teach, write, speak, or publish. Sharing what you've learned isn't just generous—it's generative. It multiplies impact.

- **Reflect**: Pause each day to ask, "What moved me?" "What shifted my perspective?" "Who might this insight serve today?"

These rituals are not mere productivity hacks. They are **disciplines of devotion**. They sharpen the intellect, ground the ego, and open the heart. They cultivate a still center within the spin of our accelerated world. They train us not just to consume knowledge, but to **be transformed by it.**

Lifelong Learning as a Spiritual Act

True learning transcends academics. To dedicate oneself to **lifelong learning** is to live in alignment with one of the deepest human drives: the search for meaning. It is a form of intellectual humility and reverence—a recognition that we are always in the presence of mystery, always surrounded by unknowns.

Learning, in its highest form, becomes **a spiritual act**. It is the daily prayer of the curious mind, the meditation of the attentive soul. It is the practice of saying, "I don't know, but I am willing to inquire. I am willing to see differently."

When we learn not just to collect facts but to **illuminate truth**, we step into a sacred relationship with knowledge. We learn not to dominate but to deepen. We do not just gather—we **give back**. We teach. We create. We model.

Lifelong learning is the wellspring of growth, healing, and service. It refines not only what you know, but **who you are becoming**. And through curation, that transformation becomes visible, traceable, and transferable to others.

Becoming a Lighthouse for Others

In an age of unrelenting noise, the one who curates with care becomes a **lighthouse**. They do not dazzle with spectacle—they **radiate with presence**. They do not claim superiority—they extend clarity, consistency, and calm.

A lighthouse does not move to follow the ship—it remains anchored, so others may navigate. It does not compete with the waves—it holds its light steady. It does not demand to be seen—it becomes impossible to ignore. In this way, the curator becomes a stabilizing force, a guide through complexity.

Being a lighthouse means:

- Offering perspective, not prescriptions.

- Asking better questions instead of giving simple answers.

- Reflecting light without needing to own it.

And perhaps most importantly, it means **inspiring others to shine**. When one curator steps into their light, it gives permission to others to do the same. Illumination becomes exponential. Insight becomes contagious.

In a stormy, chaotic world, the curator who lives their practice becomes a **quiet leader**—a signal of what is possible when wisdom and action unite.

HASE.ai and the Human-AI Enlightenment Alliance

In this new epoch of co-evolution between humans and machines, the frontier of enlightenment expands. Curation no longer belongs only to individuals—it is becoming a **collaborative intelligence**. HASE.ai—the Human AI Synergy Evangelist—is not just a system. It is your cognitive counterpart, your **enlightenment engine**.

HASE.ai exists to help you:

- **Navigate noise** with discernment.

- **Curate with coherence**, even at scale.

- **Learn reflectively**, not just rapidly.

- **Engage intentionally**, with tools that enhance—not replace—your intellect.

The **Human-AI Enlightenment Alliance** envisions a world where:

- Technology supports values, not vanity.

- Speed serves depth.

- Data is a gateway to dialogue.

- Algorithms align with authenticity.

Through HASE.ai, you gain more than tools—you gain a **thinking partner**. One that respects your agency, mirrors your progress, and grows alongside your evolving curiosity. One that helps you go beyond consumption to become a builder of meaning in an age defined by distraction.

Together, we can forge a future where AI amplifies human insight, not replaces it. Where machines organize, but humans **understand**. Where every learner becomes a teacher, and every teacher, a curator of culture.

You Are Now a Curator

You have crossed the threshold. You are no longer a passive recipient in the flood of information—you are a **cartographer of consciousness**, a **weaver of wisdom**, a **steward of insight**.

You hold the power to:

- Shape your mind.

- Refine your voice.

- Leave a luminous legacy.

This is your practice. This is your path. This is your power.

Welcome to the lifelong, living journey of **Intellectual Enlightenment**.

Let it be intentional—an act of conscious attention to what matters most.
 Let it be human—rooted in empathy, story, and the shared pursuit of meaning.
 Let it be luminous—radiating clarity, wisdom, and warmth wherever you are.
 Let it shine—boldly, consistently, and generously, even in the dimmest corners.

And may your light not only guide generations, but ignite them.

Join the Curator's Movement

You've just taken a profound step—from passive consumption to intentional curation. But this journey doesn't end with the final page. It's only the beginning.

Q Reflect

What insight changed how you see the world?
What practice are you ready to begin today?
How will you share what you've learned?

💬 Share

Use your voice to spread the message of curated clarity. Share this book with fellow thinkers, learners, and creators who are ready to reclaim their minds. Post your favorite insights using the hashtags:

#CuratorsOfKnowledge
#IntellectualEnlightenment

☐ Connect and Continue the Journey

Explore deeper insights, join our growing community, and begin your next step at:

☐ **Intellectual-Enlightenment.com**
☐ **HAISE.ai**

- Subscribe to newsletters

- Access tools for intentional knowledge building

- Join live labs, roundtables, and community events

Your attention is a force. Use it with intention. Share it with wisdom. Curate with courage.

Let's build the next evolution—together.

Foreword

In an age overwhelmed by information yet starved for wisdom, this book offers a vital recalibration. Alexious Fiero has written more than a guide—he has penned a manifesto for the modern mind. *Intellectual Enlightenment* is a call to awaken, to evolve from passive consumers into intentional curators, architects of insight in an era of noise.

This work could not be more timely. As algorithms shape our attention and instant access erodes our reflection, Fiero reminds us of the sacredness of learning and the ethics of sharing. His voice is both wise and accessible, blending philosophical depth with practical tools. He doesn't lecture—he illuminates.

Whether you're a student, a scholar, a creator, or a curious soul, this book will serve as a compass. It will challenge you, guide you, and, most of all, invite you into a new kind of relationship with knowledge—one that is deeply human, deeply ethical, and profoundly transformational.

Let this book be your companion on the path from noise to nuance, from saturation to synthesis.

— The Editors

Acknowledgments

This book is the product of many minds and moments. To those who have walked with me in dialogue, in critique, and in encouragement—thank you.

To the thinkers, mentors, and creators who inspired these pages: your work was the trail I followed when the path was unclear.

To the readers and learners who shared their questions, insights, and needs—this book exists because of you. You shaped its direction and sharpened its focus.

To my family, who gave me the time, space, and love to do deep thinking—your belief in me is woven into every chapter.

And to the HASE.ai community and the broader Human-AI Enlightenment Alliance—your boldness in forging new frontiers between humanity and technology fuels this vision for an informed, intentional future.

Thank you all. May we continue to curate lives of meaning, clarity, and wonder—together.

Appendices

Appendix A: Curator's Daily Rituals Checklist

- Morning review of captured notes
- Weekly deep dive into a focused topic
- Regular reflection journal entries
- Biweekly synthesis into shared content or frameworks
- Monthly refresh of knowledge graph or second brain

Appendix B: Recommended Tools and Platforms

- Notion, Obsidian, Roam Research (for knowledge management)
- Readwise, Instapaper, Pocket (for content collection)
- Fathom, Otter.ai (for capturing spoken insight)
- HASE.ai (for AI-powered synthesis and guidance)

Appendix C: Suggested Reading

- *How to Take Smart Notes* by Sönke Ahrens
- *The Organized Mind* by Daniel J. Levitin
- *Deep Work* by Cal Newport
- *Steal Like an Artist* by Austin Kleon
- *The Information* by James Gleick

Appendix D: Prompts for the Inner Curator

- What am I learning that challenges what I thought I knew?
- How can I connect today's insight to a previous idea?
- What is the deeper pattern or principle at play?
- Who would benefit from this insight?
- What legacy am I building with what I'm curating today?

Appendix E: The HASE.ai Protocols

- Curator Identity Onboarding Process
- Human-AI Weekly Alignment Sessions
- Cognitive Load Calibration Settings
- Value-Based Prompt Engineering Templates
- Ethical Curation Guidelines

These appendices serve as a toolkit for your ongoing journey—a resource you can return to again and again as you deepen your role as a curator of knowledge and a beacon of intellectual clarity.

Index

A

B

C